I Declare War

4 Keys to Winning the Battle with Yourself

STUDY GUIDE | 5 SESSIONS

LEVI LUSKO

with Allen Arnold

W Publishing Group

AN IMPRINT OF THOMAS NELSON

I Declare War Study Guide

© 2018 by Levi Lusko

Published in Nashville, Tennessee, by W Publishing Group, an imprint of Thomas Nelson. W Publishing Group and Thomas Nelson are registered trademarks of HarperCollins Christian Publishing, Inc.

Published in association with Wolgemuth & Associates.

Scripture quotations marked CEV are taken from the Contemporary English Version®. Copyright © 1995 American Bible Society. All rights reserved.

Scripture quotations marked MSG [or The Message] are taken from *The Message*. Copyright © by Eugene H. Peterson 1993, 1994, 1995, 1996, 2000, 2001, 2002. Used by permission of NavPress. All rights reserved. Represented by Tyndale House Publishers, Inc.

Scripture quotations marked NASB are taken from the New American Standard Bible®, Copyright © 1960, 1962, 1963, 1968, 1971, 1972, 1973, 1975, 1977, 1995 by The Lockman Foundation. Used by permission. (www.Lockman.org).

Scripture quotations marked NCV are taken from the New Century Version®. Copyright © 2005 by Thomas Nelson. Used by permission. All rights reserved.

Scripture quotations marked NIRV are taken from the Holy Bible, New International Reader's Version®. Copyright © 1996, 1998 Biblica. All rights reserved throughout the world. Used by permission of Biblica.

Scripture quotations marked NIV are taken from The Holy Bible, New International Version®, NIV®. Copyright © 1973, 1978, 1984, 2011 by Biblica, Inc.® Used by permission of Zondervan. All rights reserved worldwide. www. Zondervan.com. The "NIV" and "New International Version" are trademarks registered in the United States Patent and Trademark Office by Biblica, Inc.®

Scripture quotations marked NKJV are taken from the New King James Version®. Copyright © 1982 by Thomas Nelson. Used by permission. All rights reserved.

Scripture quotations marked NLT are taken from the Holy Bible, New Living Translation, copyright © 1996, 2004, 2015 by Tyndale House Foundation. Used by permission of Tyndale House Publishers, Inc., Carol Stream, Illinois 60188. All rights reserved.

Thomas Nelson titles may be purchased in bulk for educational, business, fundraising, or sales promotional use. For information, please e-mail SpecialMarkets@ThomasNelson.com.

ISBN 978-0-310-09487-6

First Printing September 2018 / Printed in the United States of America

CONTENTS

INTRODUCTION

I *declare war.* What images does that phrase stir up in your mind? Maybe you picture armed troops moving into position on a battlefield. Or perhaps it brings up scenes of fighter jets flying into formation for a dogfight. Or you might envision leaders of nations announcing their intention to go to war against another power—much like Franklin D. Roosevelt did after the attack on Pearl Harbor, when he said to the American people:

> Yesterday, December 7, 1941—a date which will live in infamy—the United States of America was suddenly and deliberately attacked by naval and air forces of the Empire of Japan. . . . Hostilities exist. There is no blinking at the fact that our people, our territory, and our interests are in grave danger. With confidence in our armed forces—with the unbounding determination of our people—we will gain the inevitable triumph—so help us God.[1]

Today, whether you realize it or not, you are also at war. Hostilities exist between you and your adversary. I have no doubt in my own life that the devil sends his demons to mess with me. But beyond this, I also know that I cause more than enough problems to keep myself occupied. I am my biggest enemy, and I desperately want and need to get out of my own way.

I am guessing that you can relate. I imagine that you, like me, have encountered struggles with your *thoughts* . . . or with your *words* . . . or with your *actions*. Left unchecked, these struggles will break you down—day by day—and fill your life with pain and suffering.

I was recently reminded of this truth while watching a segment on a news program about the Millennium Tower in San Francisco. Constructed in the early 2000s at a cost of $350 million, and standing at a height of 645 feet, its 58 stories boast every amenity possible to attract the tech moguls and venture capitalists of Silicon Valley. There is only one problem . . . and it is a major one: *the building is sinking.*

So far, it has sunk by seventeen inches, and it is tilting fourteen inches to the northwest. Slowly but surely, it is being swallowed up by the earth at the rate of one-and-a-half to two inches per year. The reason? Engineers failed to anchor the foundation in bedrock. The entire structure is built on concrete friction piles embedded eighty feet down into sand. But to get to the more secure layer of bedrock, workers would have had to have gone down to 200 feet.[2]

The moral of the story? If you want to go up high and withstand the stresses of this modern life, you need to build your foundation on something solid. This is exactly what Jesus said in one of his more famous parables:

These words I speak to you are not incidental additions to your life, homeowner improvements to your standard of living. They are foundational words, words to build a life on. If you work these words into your life, you are like a smart carpenter who built his house on solid rock. Rain poured down, the river flooded, a tornado hit—but nothing moved that house. It was fixed to the rock. But if you just use my words in Bible studies and don't work them into your life, you are like a stupid carpenter who built his house on the sandy beach. When a storm rolled in and the waves came up, it collapsed like a house of cards (Matthew 7:24–27 MSG).

To be fair, our lives often sway more than the Millennium Tower. We aren't confident in who we are, so we hide behind masks. We embrace wrong thoughts that lead to hurtful words, which then lead to actions we wish we could undo. We're wobbly from bad decisions. Worse, we're *sinking*. The answer to such a crisis isn't a new paint job. It's a new foundation.

Today, you need to get serious about your thoughts, words, and actions that are keeping you down. You need to name those behaviors and declare war against them if you want to overcome them. And just as in the card game War—which you probably played with your friends as a kid—your victory will be determined by laying down the right cards.

You have an enemy who wants to keep you locked into the same patterns of negative and destructive behaviors. There is no blinking at the fact that you, your territory, and your interests are in grave danger from his attacks. Your only recourse is to declare war against him and all that is holding you back—on all the darkness, the demons, the anxieties, the narcissism, the selfishness, and all your self-sabotaging ways.

It is time to rise up and fight for what matters most—winning the war within yourself.

How to Use
This Guide

The *I Declare War* video study is designed to be experienced in a group setting such as a Bible study, Sunday school class, or any small group gathering. Each session begins with a brief welcome section and several opening questions to get you thinking about the topic. You will then watch a video with Levi Lusko and jump into some directed small-group discussion. You will close each session with a time of personal reflection and prayer as a group.

Each person in the group should have his or her own copy of this study guide. You are also encouraged to have a copy of the *I Declare War* book, as reading the book alongside the curriculum will provide you with deeper insights and make the journey more meaningful. See the "For Next Week" section at the end of each between-studies section for the chapters in the book that correspond to material you and your group are discussing.

To get the most out of your group experience, keep the following points in mind. First, the real growth in this study will happen during your small-group time. This is where you will process the content of the teaching for the week, ask questions, and learn from others as you hear what God is doing in their lives. For this reason, it is important for you to be fully committed to the group and attend each session so you can build trust and rapport with the other members. If you choose to only "go through the motions," or if you refrain from participating, there is a lesser chance you will find what you're looking for during this study.

Second, remember the goal of your small group is to serve as a place where people can share, learn about God, and build intimacy and friendship. For this reason, seek to make your group a "safe place." This means being honest about your thoughts and feelings and listening carefully to everyone else's opinion. (If you are a group leader, there are additional instructions and resources in the back of the book for leading a productive discussion group.)

Third, resist the temptation to "fix" a problem someone might be having or to correct his or her theology, as that's not the purpose of your small-group time. Also, keep everything your group shares confidential. This will foster a rewarding sense of community in your group and create a place where people can heal, be challenged, and grow spiritually.

Following your group time, reflect on the material you've covered by engaging in any or all of the between-sessions activities. For each session, you may wish to complete the personal study all in one sitting or spread it out over a few days (for example, working on it a half-hour a day on different days that week). Note that if you are unable to finish (or even start!) your between-sessions personal study, you should still attend the group study video session. You are wanted and welcome at the group even if you don't have your "homework" done.

Keep in mind the videos, discussion questions, and activities are simply meant to kick-start your imagination so you are not only open to what God wants you to hear but also how to apply it to your life. As you go through this study, be watching for what God is saying to you as it relates to declaring war against your thoughts, your words, and your actions . . . and how you can rely on your "secret weapon" in the battle.

Note: If you are a group leader, there are additional resources provided in the back of this guide to help you lead your group members through the study.

It's Time to Declare War

To be prepared for war is the most effectual means of preserving peace.

GEORGE WASHINGTON

Welcome

My guess is that you are facing a situation right now for which you don't have the answers. Something that is making you feel terrified, trapped, or lonely. You feel as if you are a victim of your circumstances . . . and you don't know where to turn for help.

Perhaps it's a cycle of retaliation with your spouse that is leading to a vicious silence that no one is willing to break. You know that if something doesn't change, your marriage isn't going to last. Or maybe you're ready to quit your job because it seems your coworkers are all against you. Or it could be a struggle with your temper. You haven't crossed the line yet, but you've come close. Or the problem might be a crippling anxiety that you just can't seem to shake. You feel as if your life is spinning out of control.

The worst thing about feeling *victimized* in this way is that it's impossible to be a *victim* and a *victor* at the same time. It's time for something better in your life. In fact, as we will discuss throughout this study, *God* wants something much better for you. He wants to lead you and guide you through the problems you are facing. But the first step in this journey requires a conscious action on your part. *You have to admit the conflict is real.*

As any soldier will tell you, you can't win a war if you are unwilling to admit a conflict exists in the first place. This is why making your declaration is so important. *I declare war . . . against the cycle of retaliation . . . against my bad behaviors . . . against anxiety and depression . . . against the darkness and my self-sabotaging tendencies.*

When you declare war in this way, you are refusing to go gently into the night or to be taken without a fight. You are waging war on the version of yourself that you don't want to be. And, as you will find, there is freedom and power in making such a declaration.

Share

If you or any of your group members are just getting to know one another, take a few minutes to introduce yourselves. Then, to kick things off, discuss one of the following questions:

♣ How many people in the group have played the card game War? How does one win or lose the game? How might that apply to this study?

—or—

♣ Why did you choose to be a part of this study? What are you hoping to learn from this experience?

Read

Invite someone to read aloud the following passage. Listen for fresh insights as you hear the verses being read, and then discuss the questions that follow.

> I am the door. If anyone enters by Me, he will be saved, and will go in and out and find pasture. The thief does not come except to steal, and to kill, and to destroy. I have come that they may have life, and that they may have it more abundantly.
>
> JOHN 10:9–10 NKJV

♣ What is one key insight that stands out to you in this passage?

♣ What desire does Jesus have for your life? What desire does the enemy have for you?

♣ What promise does Jesus make to you? What is required on your part?

WATCH

Play the video for session one. As you and your group watch, use the following outline to record any thoughts or key points that stand out to you.

NOTES

All of us have a war we are fighting, and it's a war we're facing within. We are in a battle involving the thoughts we think, the words we speak, and the actions we take.

The Bible makes it clear that both God and the enemy have an agenda for our lives. Jesus wants us to experience life to the full, but the devil seeks only to steal, kill, and destroy.

Every choice we make is a door we're deciding to walk through. And we have to choose carefully, because some doors lead to life and others lead to death.

We have to discover how to stop creating problems for ourselves—to get out of our own way. It starts with us making this statement: "I declare war on my tendency to sabatoge myself."

In the words of President Teddy Roosevelt, when we choose to *fight* the battle rather than simply *talk* or *think* about it, a "wolf rises up in our heart." Once we commit ourselves to the conflict, a new courage and resolve surfaces within us.

The first three "cards" in our declaration of war involve our words, our thoughts, and our actions. The fourth represents the all-important power of the Holy Spirit.

The fourth card is critical, because we cannot win this war in our own strength. We need God to give us power, tell us who we are, and supercharge all our efforts.

Discuss

Take a few minutes with your group members to discuss what you just watched and explore these concepts together.

1. We often think of a battle as something going on around us, yet the most important war we face is the one within us. How does this struggle tend to play out in our lives?

2. Read aloud **2 Corinthians 2:9–11**. What strategies does Paul put forward in this passage on how to outwit the enemy?

3. Notice that Paul says, "We are not unaware of his schemes" (verse 11 NIV). Why is it often so hard to detect the enemy' schemes? What can help us in this regard?

4. What is your favorite part of Teddy Roosevelt's story abou the "wolf rising up in his heart"? Why?

5. How does our commitment to declare war and engage in a conflict cause a positive shift to occur within us?

6. The first three cards we will lay down in our declaration o war deal with our words, thoughts, and actions. Of thesection three, which do you struggle with the most? Why?

Pray

Wrap up your time together with prayer—simply taking a few minutes to talk with God. Here are a few ideas of what you could pray about based on what you discussed in this session:

+ Ask God to bring clarity to the specific areas he wants to transform in your lives.
+ Pray for God to strengthen you as you rise up against what's been holding you back.
+ Declare that the way things *have been* are not the way things *will be* going forward.
+ Ask for greater understanding on how your words, your thoughts, and your actions have been leading to life—or destruction—for you and those around you.
+ Declare war on your tendency to sabotage yourself.

Respond

This week, set aside some time to evaluate what you discussed with your group in this session and how you'll apply it to your life. A good place to start is to identify your primary struggles. Write them down below. Declare war on them. Remember . . . this isn't just about making a list so you can just think about or talk about the struggles. Naming your struggles is a concrete way of declaring war on the version of yourself that you don't want to be.

+ _____
+ _____
+ _____

SESSION 1

Between–Sessions Personal Study

Reflect on the material you've covered this week by engaging in any or all of the following between-sessions activities. Each day offers a short reading from *I Declare War*, along with a few reflection questions to take you deeper into the theme of this week's study. Journal or jot down your thoughts after each question. At the start of the next session, you will have a few minutes to share any insights you learned . . . but remember, the primary goal of these questions is for your own personal growth and your own private reflection.

DAY ONE:
A Maze with No Exits

There is nothing I can do to stop it.

My stomach flutters, and my skin is glistening with sweat. Thinking about all the different ways I could possibly die by my own hands, I lurch from sleep with a sickening quickness, like an unbuckled crash test dummy in a simulated collision. My mind races, and my eyes burn. The voice in my head telling me I am going to kill myself sounds like me, but it is not on my side. Helplessly I watch myself moving toward a path of self-harm—and I have no emergency brake to pull. Panicking, disoriented, and scared, I stumble out of bed and pace the hall, trying to figure out where I am and why I am so afraid.

Under my breath, I mumble a trusted Bible verse from my arsenal over and over . . . weapons I keep in my war chest for specific situations just like this. Eventually I'm able to bring down my mind's RPM from a scream to a dull roar. The fear that hung in the air like a thick, acrid smoke soon dissipates, and I start to feel like things will be all right. I peel off my T-shirt and towel off my damp skin before crawling back into bed.

Variations of this 2:00 a.m. ritual have played out as far back as I can remember. . . . The Bible calls these fits "terror by night" (Psalm 91:5 NKJV), and in the moment it feels like being locked in a maze with no exits. I don't always have suicidal thoughts; sometimes I fear harm happening to my children or making a mistake with enormous, terrible implications. For many years my fear took the form of a sense of pressure and urgency, as though I were forced to figure out a puzzle underwater, in the dark, in a language I didn't speak, with the weight of the world bearing down on me and a thousand loved ones' lives depending on my ability to do what I knew I couldn't.

♣ What is your greatest fear? Describe your first memory of being hit with this fear.

♣ Read Psalm 91:5 aloud, letting the words slowly sink in. Have you had an experience similar to what's described in this Scripture? If so, how did you respond when it occurred?

♣ The psalmist proclaimed, "With [God] on my side, I'm fearless, afraid of no one and nothing" (Psalm 27:1 MSG). When was a time you leaned into God and had victory over fear?

♣ Why do you think it is so hard to remain fearless?

DAY TWO:
WHEN FEAR STRIKES

My night terrors haven't gone away, but I have learned how to manage them better. They seem to ramp up when something big is about to happen, like when I'm facing a major opportunity or when our church is about to expand.

Unfortunately, nighttime isn't the only time my mind locks up with fear; daytime can be just as scary. Anxious thoughts, fears, worries, and the regrets that come when walking away from a conversation you wish you could do over—all can be just as difficult.

Sometimes I watch myself shifting slowly into a funk that I know will lead to unhappiness. I become like Bruce Willis in *The Sixth Sense*. I try to avoid this well-worn path that leads to nowhere. I plead with myself, *Turn around! Quit pouting. This is not the way to get what you want. Use your words and stop sulking!* But I don't seem to heed the warning, no matter how much I wave my arms and raise my voice.

This is not even to mention the addictive way I mindlessly turn to social media, online shopping, and other digital distractions when I am feeling sad, lonely, unappreciated, or bored, or when I am just avoiding working on something great. Oh, yeah—I also look to food to give me comfort when I am down. Carbs are my go-to agent for a quick hit of happiness when I am blue. The empty calories never seem to fill the emptiness in me that I am trying to shove them into, and I know I will feel worse in half an hour, but that doesn't stop me from shoveling chips into my mouth by the handful.

♣ What type of situations tend to trigger anxiety within you. Name a few of them.

♣ Do those fears seem to ramp up when something big is about to happen? If so, why do you think that's the case?

♣ Read Psalm 46:1. When you are consumed with anxiety or fear, does God feel like "a very present help" (NIV)? Why or why not?

♣ What are some ways you can replace negative thoughts with positive ones based on God's promise to be your refuge and strength?

DAY THREE:
THE WOLF WILL RISE

When you decide you're done playing the blame game and you're ready to become a victor, you will find that a wolf rises in your heart. That is how Theodore Roosevelt, the youngest person to hold the office of president, described the "power of joy in battle" that floods a person who chooses to meet the challenge spread out before him.[3] This larger-than-life president, who is literally chiseled in stone on Mount Rushmore (and is permanently one and the same with Robin Williams because of *Night at the Museum*, at least in my mind), led the Rough Riders on horseback into the battle for San Juan Hill during the Spanish-American War. Mauser machine gun bullets sprayed out from the top of the mountain, cutting down man after man, yet Teddy fought on, relentlessly urging his men forward.

In that terrible situation he crossed a barbed wire fence that lay on the battlefield and fully committed to the action before him—and at that moment a wolf rose in his heart. . . . Teddy had flipped a switch inside, and he was unstoppable in his resolve to do what was necessary. A witness said that from the instant he stepped across the wire he "became the most magnificent soldier I have ever seen."[4] A shell exploded near him, burning his skin, yet he pressed on. A stray bullet nicked his elbow, but he didn't notice. He didn't stop until the battle was won. For the rest of his life, he referred to that day, July 1, 1898, as the greatest day of his life. . . .

There is incredible power in setting all that is within you in a singular direction.

♣ What does the phase "a wolf rises in your heart" mean to you?

♣ Can you relate to this imagery? If not, how would you describe the "power of joy in battle" that floods a person the moment he or she chooses to meet a challenge?

♣ Read Joshua 1:9. God's promise to Joshua is as true for you today as it was when he spoke it to his people back then. What do these words stir in you? Why?

♣ Why is there such incredible power when you set all that is within you in a singular direction? Describe a situation where you felt courage rise once you fully committed to action.

DAY FOUR:
GOING ON THE OFFENSIVE

So much of the time, we react defensively to what comes our way. Stop letting life happen to you, and start happening to your life. Meet the enemy on your terms. Go on the offensive. Whether you are a sophomore in college or are in your sixties and contemplating life after retirement, when you decide to stare the things in the face that are holding you back, a strength will bubble up inside your chest. As twentieth-century Scottish explorer W. H. Murray wrote, "The moment one definitely commits oneself, then Providence moves too . . . raising in one's favour all manner of unforeseen incidents and meetings and material assistance, which no man could have dreamt would have come his way."[5]

Declare war, and the wolf will rise. Don't overthink it—you have time to work through all the implications. And you're not going to have to fight alone; you have an enormous amount of backup and firepower at your disposal. . . . Each session, or "card," in this study deals with a vital component of your internal struggles. And each card builds toward the most vital card—the fourth one.

It's essential you make it to the end. As good as the first three cards are, they won't matter without the all-important fourth card.

I've lived the principles I'm going to share with you. They're at play in my life right now. . . . Every manner of distraction, depression, and gloom has filled my mind the past few months. But I finally crossed the barbed wire because I know you need these concepts as much as I do.

♣ Do you tend to approach your life more *defensively* o *offensively*? Why do you think this is the case?

♣ It is easy to see yourself as *who you have been* rather tha *who you are becoming*. In what ways have you tended t view yourself through that lens?

♣ Read 2 Corinthians 5:17. How does this verse describe ho God sees you? Try describing that person below.

♣ As you approach the end of this first session, do you sens the "wolf" rising up as you consider the battle before you Why or why not?

DAY FIVE:
MAKE YOUR DECLARATION

Before we move on to the next session, it's time for you to write your specific Declaration of War in the space provided below.

Start by writing these four words: I declare war on _____. Next, underneath that phrase, list what you are declaring war against. Be specific. For example, "I declare war against <u>the darkness I feel in my life</u>." Or, "I declare war on <u>the demons that come to mess with me when I am feeling vulnerable</u>." Or, "I declare war on <u>anxiety and depression and my self-sabotaging tendencies</u>."

Don't sanitize your list. The time for half measures is over. To be clean, you must come clean. Remember, you are not entering into this battle in your own strength. So, under your declaration, describe how you are trusting God for the victory and leaning fully into his strength. Claim his protection and resolve to put on his armor (see Ephesians 6:10–20).

This doesn't have to be perfect. But you do need to be clear what you are declaring war against. Like Theodore Roosevelt, once you flip the switch inside, you too can be unstoppable in your resolve to do what is necessary. It is time for the wolf to rise up!

I DECLARE WAR ON

_____

_____

This is what I am specifically declaring war against . . .

This is how I am trusting God for the victory and relying on his strength . . .

This is how I am claiming his protection and putting on his armor . . .

For Next Week

Use the space below to write any key insights or questions from your personal study that you want to discuss at the next group meeting. In preparation for next week, review Card 1 (chapters 1–4) in *I Declare War*.

2

DECLARING WAR ON YOUR THOUGHTS

As [a man] thinks in his heart, so is he.

PROVERBS 23:7 NKJV

WELCOME

In the words of Winston Churchill, a man who knew quite a bit about war, "You must put your head into the lion's mouth if the performance is to be a success."[6] It takes courage to take that first step of putting your head in the "lion's mouth" and admitting the struggle is real. It takes strength to choose to fight rather than pretend all is well. But it is the only way for the "performance" to be a success—and for you to reach victory against your struggles.

Now that you have taken this first crucial step, it's time to flip over the first of the four cards that we will discuss in this study. It's time to declare war on our *thoughts*. Why start with our thoughts? The reason is because it is impossible for us to *live* right if we don't first *think* right. Our thoughts are invisible, but they affect everything we say and do. As one writer put it, "Be careful what you think, because your thoughts run your life" (Proverbs 4:23 NCV).

Take bad moods, for example. In my life, I remember walking to art class as a senior in high school and being in a bad mood. The class was at the end of the day, and I consoled myself by saying at least it was almost over . . . and tomorrow would be better. But the funny thing is I can't recall a single occasion when I walked *out* of art class grumpy, angry, or wound up. For forty-five minutes, we would paint, draw, or sketch. Sometimes we were even allowed to listen to music while we worked. Before I knew it, class was over and I was shuffling back on that same gravel road—but now in a completely altered state. Miraculously, the spell had lifted.

Looking back, I realize the combination of music, art, and quiet had taken me to a different place. On the way to class it had felt like the *whole* day was bad, but on the way back it felt like there were some good parts. In reality, the bad mood had only existed *in my mind*. The same is true for each of us—and that's good news, because it means we can change our lives by changing our minds. As Paul wrote, "Let God change the way you think. Then you will know how to do everything that is good and pleasing to him" (Romans 12:2 CEV).

Winning the war for our minds is a crucial first step in the battle. Today, we will look at some practical steps on how to advance against our enemy in this regard and take back any territory he has claimed in this area. We will declare war on our thoughts!

♣HARE

If you or any of your group members are just meeting for the first time, take a few minutes to introduce yourselves and share any insights you have from last week's personal study. Next, to kick things off for the group time, discuss one of the following questions:

♣ Think about a few times recently when you have been in a bad mood. What put you in that state? What ultimately lifted you out of it?

—*or*—

♣ Think about this statement: *You are not the thoughts you think.* Is that an easy or difficult truth for you to embrace? Why?

READ

Invite someone to read aloud the following passage. Listen for fresh insight and to share any new thoughts with the group through the questions that follow.

> For though we live in the world, we do not wage war as the world does. The weapons we fight with are not the weapons of the world. On the contrary, they have divine power to demolish strongholds. We demolish arguments and every pretension that sets itself up against the knowledge of God, and we take captive every thought to make it obedient to Christ.
>
> 2 CORINTHIANS 10:3–5 NIV

♣ **What is one key insight that stands out to you in this passage?**

♣ **What does Paul say in this passage about the way we wage war against our enemy?**

♣ **What does it mean to "take captive" every thought and make it obedient to Jesus?**

WATCH

Play the video for session two. As you and your group watch, use the following outline to record any thoughts or key points that stand out to you.

NOTES

Step one in winning the war within is realizing that thoughts full of insecurities lead to a miserable life. Always focusing on ourselves and our problems will only bring us misery.

The payoff for focusing on ourselves, living out of our insecurities, and pretending we're something we're not, is that we end up feeling like a stranger in our own soul.

Negative thoughts will pop into our heads, but that doesn't mean we have to dwell on them. Martin Luther said, "You cannot prohibit the birds from flying over your head; but make sure they . . . do not build a nest in your hair."

Step two in winning the war with your thoughts is installing checkpoints in your mind. Only let in things that are true, noble, pure, of good report, virtuous, and praiseworthy.

Step three in winning the war with your thoughts is knowing it's never too late to change course. God has brand-new mercies for you tomorrow . . . and for you right now.

Bad things happen when we put a negative where there should be a positive—whether with a car battery or our minds. We can't lead a positive life through negative thoughts.

Discuss

Take a few minutes with your group members to discuss what you just watched and explore these concepts together.

1. Can you remember any hurtful words that were spoken over or about you as a child? How have those words or names stuck with you in your adult years?

2. We talk to ourselves more than any other person, and often the words we speak are unkind and untrue. How might such internal thoughts fuel our insecurities? How do such thoughts, left unchecked, make us more miserable?

3. Read aloud **Matthew 10:39** and **Luke 9:24**. What is the payoff for living out of our insecurities? How does this lead to us putting on masks to hide our God-given identity?

4. Read aloud **Matthew 4:1–11.** When Jesus was in the wilderness, the enemy attacked with three temptations in the hopes of getting Jesus to agree to his way of thinking. How did Jesus stay strong in this battle? How can we use the same approach?

5. Is it possible to be in control of our thoughts? Why or why not?

6. Read aloud **Philippians 4:8.** What advice does Paul give in this passage? What steps are involved in the process of installing "checkpoints" in our minds?

PRAY

Wrap up your time together with prayer—simply taking a few minutes to talk with God. Here are a few ideas of what you could pray about based on what you discussed in this session:

- ♦ Ask God to reveal the negative self-talk that clutters your thoughts.
- ♦ Pray for the wisdom to control your thoughts.
- ♦ Thank God that his mercies are new every morning and every moment of the day.
- ♦ Ask God to help you embrace your true identity rather than your insecurities.
- ♦ Declare that you are not your thoughts.
- ♦ Ask God to help free you from the masks you wear.
- ♦ Praise God that he works all things for your good (see Romans 8:28).

RESPOND

In Colossians 3:1, Paul writes, "Set your hearts on things above, where Christ is, seated at the right hand of God" (NIV). The word *set* is a verb. It means *you* decide what you're going to think. Rather than letting any thought make itself at home, you choose to set your heart and mind on things above. That's positive thinking at its finest. This week, try to consciously set your mind on the things that God wants you to think about. Remember that "every train is a thought"—and before jumping on one, you want to make sure it's going to where you want to be.

SESSION 2

BETWEEN–SESSIONS PERSONAL STUDY

Reflect on the material you've covered this week by engaging in any or all of the following between-sessions activities. Journal or jot down your thoughts after each question, and write down any key insights that you want to discuss at next week's group meeting.

DAY ONE:
SIXTEEN SUNRISES A DAY

This day is spoiled. I'll just have to try again tomorrow. You've felt that way, haven't you? As though so much of the day has been wasted that there's no use trying to make good decisions. . . . Where did we get the idea that one bad decision must be followed by another? Maybe it comes from failing to understand the true meaning of an often-quoted verse written by the prophet Jeremiah in the book of Lamentations:

> Because of the LORD's great love we are not consumed,
>   for his compassions never fail.
> They are new every morning;
>   great is your faithfulness (3:22–23 NIV).

What a Bible verse *doesn't* mean is as important as what it *does*. Jeremiah isn't saying that a new morning is the only time you have the opportunity to receive mercy; there isn't anything mystical attached to the clock striking midnight. . . .

Rather, what Jeremiah emphasizes is that you always have a new shot—because God is that good. You have the option to go to him morning, noon, and night—once a day, nine times a day, every hour if you need to—and claim the help you need for the present struggle you are facing. Hebrews 4:16 says, "So let us boldly approach God's throne of grace. Then we will receive mercy. We will find grace to help us when we need it" (NIRV). You don't have to wait for the start of day; you can seek the grace when you need it.

Astronauts on the International Space Station orbit Earth every ninety minutes, which means they can watch the sun rise and set sixteen times a day. . . . The picture of an astronaut siting in the Cupola, watching the sun rise and set sixteen times in one day through the enormous window, is key for you to remember as you lean in to the reset God wants to give you: as the heavens are high above the earth, so God's ways are past finding out (see Isaiah 55:9 and Romans 11:33). The higher you go, the more sun rises there are.

You needn't write off a day that has been tainted. You can start over on the spot. . . . There are brand new mercies waiting for you. Only pride and silliness allow a bad decision to turn into a bad day and make you defer until tomorrow what you need to do right now.

♣ Recall a time you wrote a day off because of a bad decision or untrue thought. Write about that situation below.

♣ Do you find it difficult to ask God for grace and mercy after you've blown it? Why or why not?

♣ Write Lamentations 3:22–23 in the space below, but replace the word *we* with *I* to make it more personal. What phrase is the most comforting to you? Why?

♣ Read Hebrews 4:16. What promise are you given in this verse? How does the thought of being offered unlimited new beginnings change how you view any one setback?

DAY TWO:
REJOICE ALWAYS?

"Rejoice always" (1 Thessalonians 5:16 NIV). . . . Personally, I think that this tiny, little, two-word-long verse is one of the most difficult things we are told to do in all of Scripture. Rejoice *always*? Think about that: not some of the time or when things are going great, but *always*.

Paul tells us specifically that ever-present joy is a part of God's plan for our lives: "Rejoice always, pray without ceasing, in everything give thanks; for *this is the will of God in Christ Jesus for you*" (1 Thessalonians 5:16–18 NKJV, emphasis added).

Why is it important to God that you rejoice all the time, pray frequently, and stay thankful? Because it is impossible to do those things and be negative at the same time. When you feel like complaining, see yourself acting selfishly, or find yourself slipping into a bad mood, shoot a prayer to God that is full of joy and gratitude instead. Setting your mind on things above you is declaring war on low-level thinking.

The fact that it is God's will for you to be positive doesn't make it easy. . . . If you think, *I can't wait until I mature so this won't be an issue anymore*, you're setting yourself up for disappointment. There is truth to the expression "new levels, new devils." If anything, the battle grows more complex as you progress in your spiritual journey, because the more you do, the more the enemy will try to stop you.

♣ **Read Romans 7:15–20. How can you relate to Paul's words in this passage? When was a specific time that you felt "I do not understand what I do"?**

♣ Do you believe you have the power to choose which thoughts
   win? Why or why not?

♣ Write out 1 Thessalonians 5:16–18 in the space below and
   underline the words that are most relevant to where you are
   now. What times do you struggle the most to rejoice? Why?

♣ In hard times, what would it look like to set your mind on
   things above?

♣ As you progress in your spiritual journey, the battle often
   heats up. How does this motivate you to get more serious
   now in the fight to protect your thoughts?

DAY THREE:
Good Times

In the book *Extreme Ownership: How US Navy SEALs Lead and Win*, the authors, two former Navy SEALs, tell of a phrase that they have made a ritual. No matter what happens to them in the midst of all manner of madness coming their way, they choose to think in response, *Good times*. Regardless of how unexpected, inopportune, or inconvenient the task in front of them, they allow themselves only the response of *Good times*.[7] They trust the plan and each other, which gives them confidence and assurance in moving forward. That response puts them in the proper frame of mind to stay strong and increases their effectiveness. In essence, they are taking a potentially negative situation and see it from a different perspective. . . . Psychologists call this tactic *cognitive restructuring*. It allows them then to be on their toes and not on their heels as they move forward.

I dare you to try it.

Dishwasher broken? *Good. Now I'll get some time to think and listen to a podcast while I wash dishes by hand.*

It's raining again? *Good. I love the smell of rain. . . .*

The company is cutting back on hours? *Good. I have dreamed for a long time of figuring out a way to make money online, and now I have the push to make it happen. . . .*

The way to use the word *good* that will cause the wolf to rise in your heart isn't to say that the bad thing is good—but to believe that goodness will be the end result. Your pain is just a scene; it's not the entire movie. It's a chapter, not the book. David, a Navy SEAL of the Old Testament, focused on goodness this way when he wrote, "I would have lost heart, unless I had believed that I would see the goodness of the LORD in the land of the living" (Psalm 27:13 NKJV).

♣ Try the "cognitive restructuring" approach of the Navy SEALs to see a current problem from a different perspective. First, write the specific issue down. Next, reframe the situation by describing how good might come from it.

♣ Read Genesis 50:1–26. How does Joseph's response to his brothers in verse 20 influence your thinking about God's ability to reshape the bad in your life into something good?

♣ Read Psalm 27:13. When was a time that you, like David, would have lost heart unless you had confidence you would "see the goodness of the LORD"?

♣ Is it a struggle for you to believe goodness will be the end result to your story, especially while in this current chapter of life? If so, write a note to God below. Be honest if you are losing hope and ask for eyes to see how future good can come from the current bad.

DAY FOUR:
Mask On, Mask Off

Here is my confession: I care what other people think about me way too much, and I really want to be noticed and accepted. I want other people to like me because I have trouble liking myself. I need others to validate me. So many of my life's problems have come from a longing to be in the "in circle" and have a seat at that table. To be liked, celebrated, approved. . . .

Insecurity is a lack of confidence. It comes from uncertainty about your worth, value, or place in the world. Insecurity is believing that you aren't enough—pretty enough, rich enough, strong enough, smart enough—and that you don't have what it takes, that you aren't one of the cool kids, that the lies and harsh words people have spoken over your life are true. . . . As a result, we hide behind defense mechanisms that, like masks, cover our true selves. . . .

The payoff for wearing a mask is being stuck in it. If you get the job with the mask, you have to wear the mask every day at work. If you get the relationship with the mask, you have to wear the mask whenever you're with that person. . . . If you fake it, you have to keep faking it. . . .

The good news for us insecure, mask-wearing phonies is that we can choose to take the mask off. That's scary, I know. You might have been wearing one so long you don't know what life would look like without it, but let me tell you: it looks like freedom.

♣ Read Mark 8:34–38. Jesus asks how it profits us to gain the whole world if we end up losing our soul in the process. When we allow the world to tell us who we are, we lose an essential part of our being. What have you traded in exchange for praise or acceptance of others?

♣ Insecurity is believing you aren't enough—pretty enough, rich enough, strong enough, smart enough. It is seeing yourself as damaged goods and thinking that if people really knew you, they wouldn't accept you. Where do you most struggle with insecurity?

♣ What mask do you wear to try to compensate for this insecurity? Try to remember what first caused you to feel that way. Write it down. Can you now release the situation to God and ask for his healing in that area of your life?

♣ Read Psalm 139:14. What does this verse tell you about the way God sees you? How should that affect the way you see youself?

DAY FIVE:
THE CURE FOR INSECURITY

The cure for insecurity is understanding your true identity. When the Old Testament judge Gideon doubted himself and tried to put on a mask, God told him he was a mighty man of valor so he would know his true identity, trust in God, and accomplish great things (see Judges 6:12). For this reason, God refused to let Gideon fight the Midianites with the 32,000 soldiers he marshaled, insisting instead that he fight with a meager 300 by his side as he faced off against an army of 100,000 plus. The soldiers he had amassed had become another mask, but God dismantled it to get him out from what he was hiding behind. . . .

When you know who you are, it doesn't matter what you are not.

You are loved by God. That's why he made you, why he saved you. Why he shed the blood of his Son and filled you with his Spirit. Why he gave you a calling. You're loved by God! You don't need approval from anyone else, because the only likes that really matter come from heaven—and they are already yours.

God didn't get stuck with you; he chose you. You weren't a white elephant gift; God picked you knowing your faults and the skeletons in your closet. He's never been disgusted or surprised or shocked by anything you've done.

Whenever you find yourself thinking, *I don't. I can't. I'm not*, respond right back: *I do. I am. I have. I can—because I'm loved by God!*

You are not your career; you are not your collection of shoes or followers; you are not your car or your job or the table you sit at in the school cafeteria. Instead, put your value in being God's daughter or son, in being loved by him.

♣ Paul says, "Let's just go ahead and be what we were made to be, without enviously or pridefully comparing ourselves with each other, or trying to be something we aren't" (Romans 12:5–6 MSG). Why is it hard to let go of what you are not?

♣ Read Judges 6:11–40. How did God peel away the masks Gideon was relying on so Gideon could see his true identity: a mighty man of valor?

♣ Your true identity is determined by God, not the world. Describe what your God-given identity looks like. Start this way: "No matter how I feel, God has made me to be . . ."

♣ The only way to get to victory is through vulnerability. What are a few practical ways to embrace who you are as you begin the journey to become who you were born to be?

FOR NEXT WEEK

Use the space below to write any key insights or questions from your personal study that you want to discuss at the next group meeting. In preparation for next week, review Card 2 (chapters 5–7) in *I Declare War*.

DECLARING WAR
ON YOUR WORDS

The tongue has the power of life and death.

PROVERBS 18:21 NIV

WELCOME

Experts agree the Great Fire of London was a disaster just waiting to happen. Back in 1666, the city was primarily comprised of houses made of oak timber. Some of the poorer houses had walls covered with tar, which kept out the rain but made them extremely flammable. Complicating matters was the fact that the houses were crowded together. It took only a few stray sparks from the oven of the king's baker one evening to start the blaze that would eventually consume 13,000 houses, 90 churches, and leave 100,000 people homeless.[8]

One writer stated, "Death and life are in the power of the tongue, and those who love it will eat its fruit" (Proverbs 18:21 NKJV). Your tongue is a small and seemingly insignificant part of you, but if you don't keep it under control, it can be like that stray spark from the oven—capable of destruction on a massive scale. It will steer where you go, what you do, and how people react to you. This is why we now need to flip over the second card in our deck and declare war on our *words*.

The Bible is clear that your words have power. This includes what you speak to others, what you speak to yourself, what you speak about your life, and what you speak when you are afraid. Your words have the power of *death* and *life*—like a tiny nuclear reactor capable of both lighting up a town and demolishing a city. "Those who guard their lips preserve their lives, but those who speak rashly will come to ruin" (Proverbs 13:3 NIV).

Tragically, words are like toothpaste. Once they're out of the tube, there's no putting them back in. It's like a story I read about Orville Wright. He was heartsick over the use of airplanes—which he and his brother had invented—to drop bombs in World War II. It disturbed him to know he had created something that had been used to cause so much harm. But he didn't regret the invention. He knew there was no going back—what was done was done. And he also knew that his invention had been used for great good. He was reassured by the belief that *all things* that can do much evil can also do great good.[9]

So, in this session, I want you to wage war on the words you speak. I challenge you to not only make your thoughts subject to Christ but to make your words subject to his authority. After all, if he is the Lord of your *life*, he must be the Lord of your *lips* as well.

SHARE

Begin your group time by inviting anyone to share his or her insights from last week's personal study. Next, to kick things off, discuss one of the following questions:

♣ How do you respond to the idea that your words have the power of life and death? What does this say about the importance of your words?

—*or*—

♣ When was a time you said something that you wished you could take back? What happened as a result?

READ

Invite someone to read aloud the following passage. Listen for fresh insight and to share any new thoughts with the group through the questions that follow.

> When we put bits into the mouths of horses to make them obey us, we can turn the whole animal. Or take ships as an example. Although they are so large and are driven by strong winds, they are steered by a very small rudder wherever the pilot wants to go. Likewise, the tongue is a small part of the body, but it makes great boasts. Consider what a great forest is set on fire by a small spark.
>
> JAMES 3:3–5 NIV

♣ What key point is James driving home through his multiple illustrations?

♣ Small sparks can create huge forest fires and even burn down huge cities. What is an example of how our words can do the same?

♣ Why do you think it's so hard to contain or control the words that come from such a relatively small part of our body—the tongue?

WATCH

Play the video for session three. As you and your group watch, use the following outline to record any thoughts or key points that stand out to you.

NOTES

Our words have incredible power. [Our tongue] is a small part of us, but it steers all of where we go. This is why we need to be aware of the impact our words have on those who hear them.

Our words can be like a fire that warms others. Or it can be a wildfire that destroys them. The choice is up to us on how we will use them.

Step one in winning the war for our words is to remember we can change the way we feel if we change the words we speak.

Step two in winning the war for our words is to recognize we don't have to say everything we feel like saying. We've been made in God's image and have the power of choice.

Step three in winning the war for our words is to understand the words we speak over others can alter the course of their lives. With one sentence we can encourage someone or speak something that lingers like a burr in his or her shoe.

As we consider our words, we need to think about what we want our final words to be on this earth. If we belong to Jesus, our last words here will be followed by our first words in heaven.

Discuss

Take a few minutes with your group members to discuss what you just watched and explore these concepts together.

1. Read aloud **Matthew 8:13**. What was Jesus essentially saying to the centurion about his words? What does that say about the power of our speech?

2. Do you believe you can actually change the way you feel b
changing the words you speak? If so, give an example whe
you've experienced this. If not, why not?

3. Read aloud **Ephesians 4:29**. What instruction does Paul giv
us in this passage? How have you used your words recentl
to build up (bless) or tear down (curse) others?

4. We don't have to say everything we feel—we have the powe
of choice. Before speaking, how often do you ask yourself
there is alignment between what you're about to say and wh
you want the outcome of the conversation to be? Explain.

5. What person has spoken positive words over you? How hav
those encouraging words altered the course of your life?

6. Read aloud **Psalm 90:12**. How would keeping in mind that w
only have so many words to speak make us wiser with our word

PRAY

Wrap up your time together with prayer—simply taking a few minutes to talk with God. Here are a few ideas of what you could pray about based on what you discussed in this session:

- ◆ Ask God to remind you that your words are powerful.
- ◆ Give thanks that you can change the way you feel by changing your words.
- ◆ Ask God to help you hold your tongue at times when it is best to remain silent.
- ◆ Pray that no corrupting words come out of your mouth.
- ◆ Thank God for the gift he has given to name things and ask for his help in using this power for good.
- ◆ Declare your desire to speak words of life all the days of your life.

RESPOND

Imagine you are in the final moments of your life. Your loved ones are gathered around you. You have something to say to them, and they are listening. What do you want those last words to be? Don't just think them—write them down below. Then speak these "future" words aloud. As you do, consider whether you are saying similar words to those you love *right now*.

SESSION 3

BETWEEN–SESSIONS PERSONAL STUDY

Reflect on the material you've covered this week by engaging in any or all of the following between-sessions activities. Journal or jot down your thoughts after each question, and write down any key insights that you want to discuss at next week's group meeting.

DAY ONE:
NAMING RIGHTS

The first job God gave humans was to speak a word over something he made: "Now the Lord God had formed out of the ground all the wild animals and all the birds in the sky. He brought them to the man to see what he would name them; and whatever the man called each living creature, that was its name" (Genesis 2:19 NIV).

Did you catch that? Whatever man called the animal, that was its name. Adam's job was to speak, and what he spoke stuck. You have the same job. God brings to you a day, and your job is to give it a name—to declare something over it. Whatever you call it will stick.

Consider the implications . . . you trudge to the bathroom, keeping your eyes narrowed as you flip on the lights. You turn on the faucet and splash cold water on your face. . . . Then comes the moment of truth, as for the first time today you pull your hands away and look at yourself in the mirror.

What do you see looking back at you? What do you choose to say in response to the person you see in the glass?

I am beautiful or I am ugly?

I am valuable or I am not worthy of love?

I am going to have a tremendous day or I am so behind already.

Whatever you say over what you see, that is what it is called.

Maybe, like me, you have gotten so good at listening to yourself that you have forgotten to speak to yourself. It's easy to drift along with the speakers of your soul blasting the play-by-play commentary of your naturally negative self. It's time you fire yourself as your personal critic and rehire yourself as a coach. You can alter how you feel through changing the way you speak.

♣ **Read Genesis 2:19–20. When God granted man the right to name the animals, what do you think he was trying to teach us?**

♣ What names have you been declaring over yourself and your days?

♣ Going forward, do you sense the need to rename specific things you've negatively named? If so, give an example.

♣ Imagine you've just fired yourself as your personal critic and rehired yourself as a coach. The first assigment you give yourself is to alter how you feel through changing the way you speak. How would that transform your words . . . and your world?

DAY TWO:
If You Say So

Your speech can create, tear down, build, heal, or hurt.

When God hears you speak about your meeting as terrible, your car as crappy, your kids as ungrateful, your husband as lazy, your town as small, your house as cramped, his response is: *If you say so*. Because of the power he put into your tongue when he made you, he will allow the labels you speak into existence to stick. Consequently, you will have a terrible experience in your meeting, an unenjoyable ride in your crappy car. And you will find in your husband and kids a thousand examples of laziness and ingratitude. Your house will indeed shrink around you, as will the suddenly claustrophobic town you are trapped in. You will feel how you speak and find what you seek.

On the other hand, you can choose to talk about the meeting as one that will be challenging but important, full of opportunities to solve problems. You can choose to talk about how you are grateful to have a car, and how you are happy that your husband works hard to provide for your family, and how your children are going to learn gratitude from your example. That reminds you that you are thankful you don't live in that tiny studio apartment anymore, and while your current town may not be Los Angeles, it's charming in its own way. God's response to this new way of speaking is the same: *If you say so*.

Your words can unlock a life you love or one you loathe. It is up to you whether the self-fulfilling prophecies you articulate become a delight or a dungeon.

♣ Ephesians 4:29 gives us this warning about words: "Say only what helps, each word a gift" (MSG). Would others mostly describe your words as a *gift* or a *wrecking ball*? Why?

♣ When God hears you speak about something as terrible, his response is, *If you say so.* Because of the power he put into your tongue when he made you, he will allow the labels you speak into existence to stick. What would you like to label differently given this truth? Why?

♣ What is one situation where you've pronounced something in your life as good—and God has blessed it by responding, *If you say so?*

♣ Read Proverbs 25:11. Why do you think the writer used this particular imagery to convey the incredible worth of well-timed words?

DAY THREE:
Faith Is the Password

One of my favorite Bible stories illustrates the capacity your words have to set the tone for your faith and for your future. A centurion—an officer in the Roman army in charge of a hundred men—came to Jesus for help because his servant was seriously ill. . . .

The words he used show that he considers the young man to be like a son to him: "Lord, my servant is at home paralyzed, dreadfully tormented" (Matthew 8:6 NKJV). . . . Jesus immediately agreed to come to the man's home to treat his servant. But the centurion protested that there was no need for Jesus to enter his home. . . . Instead, the centurion trusted that Jesus's words would be enough: "Only speak a word, and my servant will be healed" (verse 8 NKJV). His logic is sound. If Jesus was the Word, all he needed to do was speak the word, and the servant would be fine. The creation has no choice but to respond to the Creator.

The centurion's faith astonished Jesus: "When Jesus heard it, He marveled" (verse 10 NKJV). . . . Jesus had never performed a miracle in the way this man was suggesting. Until this point, he had always been physically present when he healed people; he had touched them or prayed over them or rubbed mud in their eyes. What the centurion suggested was a long-distance miracle, which suggest a whole other level of faith in Jesus.

Jesus's response to the centurion included three incredible words that held great promise . . . "as you have believed, so *let it be* done for you" (verse 13 NKJV, emphasis added). . . . Faith is the password that unlocks God's power. Jesus said, "If you have faith as a mustard seed, you will say to this mountain, 'Move from here to there,' and it will move; and nothing will be impossible for you" (Matthew 17:20 NKJV).

The Roman soldier had enough faith to ask for a long-distance miracle, and as a result, Jesus granted his request. He received a miracle because he had faith that made Jesus marvel. Your goal should be to use your words in such a way that they bless the heart of God, inspire faith in those around you, and make life better for those who are hurting.

♣ What most stands out to you about the story of the Roman centurion's encounter with Jesus in Matthew 8? Why?

♣ "The creation has no choice but to respond to the Creator." What does this phrase mean—both in the story of the centurion and in your own life story?

♣ Jesus marveled at the centurion's great faith. Have you given Jesus a reason to marvel at your faith? If not, how might you ask him to make the impossible possible in your life?

♣ In what ways can you use your words to bless the heart of God, inspire faith in those around you, and make life better for those who are hurting? Be specific.

DAY FOUR:
THE COST OF WRATH

There is a cost to being rough. It may get you what feels good in the moment, but it will be at the expense of what you actually want. Being rude is not cheap; it's expensive.

Deep down, you know this. Even while you are sassing your parents, being sarcastic with your spouse, or spouting off at the customer service person who is high on condescension but low on customer service, you know you are making the problem worse—but in those moments, you don't care. . . .

Soon the situation escalates beyond whatever the original problem was. Instead of dialing down the intensity, you raise it to a whole new level; instead of diffusing the stress, you radiate it back to the source that sent it.

Proverbs 30:32 advises, "If you have been foolish in exalting yourself, or if you have devised evil, put your hand on your mouth" (NKJV). (That right there is some good relationship advice. How much better would your life be if you got better at putting your hand on your mouth?) "For as the churning of milk produces butter, and ringing the nose produces blood, so the forcing of wrath produces strife" (verse 33 NKJV).

The forcing of wrath in a relationship is, every single time, going to lead to strife. And you're like, *Of course. Ugh, Obvious, right?* And yet, why do we walk away surprised when people's noses are bleeding—ours and theirs—and act mystified as to what happened? . . .

Usually in those moments we say to ourselves, *Well, that wasn't my intention.* Right? We use our intentions to excuse what we actually did.

But here's a beautiful, life-changing truth: your intentions don't matter; your behavior does. No one can hear what you

wanted to say; we hear only what you said. The impact you
have on the world is what you're accountable for.

♣ Think of a time when being rude was more costly than
you imagined. What did you learn about the power of your
words from that experience?

♣ Write out Proverbs 30:32 below. What about this verse most
stands out to you? Why?

♣ Have you ever used your intentions to excuse what you actually said? If so, describe that time.

♣ No one can hear what you wanted to say; they can only hear
what you *actually* said. Do you tend to feel accountable for
the impact of your words? Why or why not?

DAY FIVE:
Break Free from Button Pushers

I've come up with a four-part matrix that enables me to slow down when I'm feeling keyed up. . . . I highly recommend that the first few times you use it, you physically draw it and fill it in, because it will force you to cool down. Eventually, you'll be able to do it in your mind in real time, and it will give you the freedom to not say everything you feel like saying.

First, draw a cross, and in the top quadrants, from left to right, put the words *Analyze* and *Extrapolate*, leaving a good amount of space below them. In the bottom quadrants, write the words *Prioritize* and *Navigate*. Under Analyze, write: *I want to . . .* and then write exactly what you want to say or do because of being angry, sad, or rejected. . . .

After you analyze the situation, the next step is to Extrapolate—*if I do this, then this will happen*. Play out the scenario, and take it to its logical end. . . . It's incredibly helpful to understand the implications of a given decision before taking action.

The third step is to Prioritize. Write: *What I really want to happen is* _____. . . . What do you want to be the outcome of this situation? How do you want this night to end? If you were to come up with the storyboard for this situation, what's the last pane of the comic? . . .

The last and most important step is to Navigate. In this quadrant, write: *What I need to do to get there is* _____. What can you do to get you from where you are to where you want to be? Pro-tip: it will often be the opposite of whatever you started out feeling like doing. . . .

Understanding these four steps and applying them will help you immensely. So take a few minutes to complete the exercise on the following pages.

INSTRUCTIONS

1. **Analyze:** Using the diagram on the facing page, complete this sentence with exactly what you want to say or do. Don't run from your emotions; study them.

2. **Extrapolate:** Play out the scenario to its logical end. It's incredibly helpful to understand the implications of a given decision before taking action.

3. **Prioritize:** What do you want to be the outcome of this situation? What is the final scene you want to have happen before the credits role?

4. **Navigate:** This is the solution that brings words of life rather than death (see Proverbs 18:21). What can you do to get you from where you are to where you want to be?

ANALYZE

I want to . . .

EXTRAPOLATE

If I do this, then this
will happen . . .

What I really want
to happen is . . .

What I need to do
to get there is . . .

PRIORITIZE

NAVIGATE

For Next Week

Use the space below to write any key insights or questions from your personal study that you want to discuss at the next group meeting. In preparation for next week, review Card 3 (chapters 8–10) in *I Declare War*.

DECLARING WAR
ON YOUR ACTIONS

Wise choices will watch over you.
Understanding will keep you safe.

PROVERBS 2:11 NLT

Welcome

Even the smallest decisions you make can lead to great things in your life. Take the case of artist David Choe, who in 2005 was asked to paint the offices of a startup company in Palo Alto, California. Choe's pricetag for the project was $60,000, so the fledling company offered to pay his fee in shares of stock. Although Choe didn't really get the company's business model, he agreed to the deal. The name of the startup was Facebook. Seven years later, Choe's decision to take the stock led to a windfall in the nature of $200 million.[10]

The philosopher Will Durant observed, "We are what we repeatedly do."[11] Every action we take forms a pattern for how we will behave in the future—and over time, those actions can have a great impact. Even seemingly insignificant actions such as the way we respond to our moods, the feelings we act on, and the way we treat those in authority can be like water dripping on a rock. Eventually, the water will dissolve the minerals in the rock and wear down a groove into it. Given enough time, it can become the Grand Canyon.

I came across a fascinating and alarming essay in the book *Everyday Emotional Intelligence* that claimed: "Research suggests that our range of emotional skills is relatively set by our mid-20s and that our accompanying behaviors are, by that time, deep-seated habits. And therein lies the rub: the more we act a certain way—be it happy, depressed, or cranky—the more the behavior becomes engrained in our brain circuitry, and the more we will continue to feel and act that way."[12] Notice that last point: *our behaviors become locked in our brains.*

The same drip of water that can wear down the minerals in a rock can also build up huge columns in caves known as stalactites and stalagmites. Each drip of water—like each action in our lives—leaves behind a deposit that can build up over time. Once formed, those formations are difficult to break. This is why it is absolutely code-blue critical that the wolf rises in our hearts and we declare war on the version of ourselves that we don't want to be.

You haven't got a moment to lose in this effort. You can't afford to put off change until tomorrow. Your habits are forming and hardening as we speak. It's time to turn over the third card and declare war on your actions.

SHARE

Begin your group time by inviting anyone to share his or her insights from last week's personal study. Next, to kick things off, discuss one of the following questions:

♣ What are some actions you have taken that seemed insignificant at the time but led to big changes in your life? What did you learn from these times?

—*or*—

♣ What are some of your daily habits that you do on autopilot? What is one example of a mindless routine from your day that's worth rethinking?

READ

Invite someone to read aloud the following passage. Listen for fresh insight and to share any new thoughts with the group through the questions that follow.

> Therefore, prepare your minds for action, keep sober in spirit, fix your hope completely on the grace to be brought to you at the revelation of Jesus Christ. As obedient children, do not be conformed to the former lusts which were yours in your ignorance, but like the Holy One who called you, be holy yourselves also in all your behavior.
>
> 1 PETER 1:13–15 NASB

♣ **What is one key insight that stands out to you in this passage?**

♣ **What are some ways that you prepare your mind for action? Which have been the most effective for you? Why?**

♣ **What does this verse say about how followers of Christ should act and behave?**

WATCH

Play the video for session four. As you and your group watch, use the following outline to record any thoughts or key points that stand out to you.

NOTES

Our lives are automated in a literal sense. Our lives are built up of habits—what we do again and again—and what we do repeatedly, we eventually become.

Step one in winning the war for our actions is to learn to feel our feelings. Pausing between a desire to do something and actually taking the action breaks the negative cycle of automating our actions based on feelings.

Step two in winning the war for our actions is to start before we're ready. We may never feel completely ready for the significant things God wants us to do.

When we wake up in the morning, we need to do the most significant tasks first. Perseverance leads to the seeds we plant in our lives becoming strong trees.

Step three in winning the war for our actions is to foster the discipline of putting on our game face. How we carry ourselves—our posture, our body language—is important.

The "game before the game" involves the work we do to prepare ourselves for action. We choose what we will do in response to different situations before we ever get into them.

Discuss

Take a few minutes with your group members to discuss wha you just watched and explore these concepts together.

1. What are some habits that you're glad you started? How hav you seen the positive impact of those actions in your life an the lives of others?

2. Read aloud **James 2:14–17**. What does this passage say abou the importance of our actions? What are some habits tha you need to begin?

3. What does it mean to "put on your game face"? What doe that look like in your life?

4. Read aloud **Joel 3:10**. How does declaring this truth impac your sense of boldness? How might it change your dail decisions?

5. Moses spent forty years wandering around the desert as a shepherd before he was ready for the forty years of leading God's people. What season of life are you in currently? What is God calling you to do in this season?

6. When Peter says, "prepare your minds for action" (1 Peter 1:13 NASB), he indicates you can actively choose how you're going to respond to situations before you get into them. What is an example where you've done this? What was the outcome?

𝒫RAY

Wrap up your time together with prayer—simply taking a few minutes to talk with God. Here are a few ideas of what you could pray about based on what you discussed in this session:

- ◆ Pray for God to prepare your mind for action.
- ◆ Lean in to God's strength to start what he calls you to do . . . even before you feel ready to do it.
- ◆ Ask God for the courage to step into each day filled with worship rather than fear.
- ◆ Declare in your heart that you are who God says you are—the son or daughter of the King, filled with the same Spirit that raised Christ from the dead.
- ◆ Thank God that you can do all things through Christ who strengthens you.

Respond

British evangelist Charles Spurgeon once said, "The way to do a great deal is to keep on doing a little. The way to do nothing at all is to be continually resolving that you will do everything." The concept is brilliant. If your focus is on doing everything for everyone, you will end up doing nothing. But if you can prioritize some small steps you can take *right now*, they will lead you to the great things you eventually want to achieve. So, this week, your challenge is to identify some small positive behaviors that you can start doing right now and put them into action. This likely means *starting before you feel ready*. But it's a crucial step in declaring war on your actions.

SESSION 4

BETWEEN-SESSIONS PERSONAL STUDY

Reflect on the material you've covered this week by engaging in any or all of the following between-sessions activities. Journal or jot down your thoughts after each question, and write down any key insights that you want to discuss at next week's group meeting.

DAY ONE:
EXAMINE YOUR HABITS

According to research from Duke University, about 45 percent of our actions each day are habits.[13] That means that close to half of your life you're not actually thinking carefully about what you are doing but are running through an automated ritual baked in to your being. . . .

It's critical to examine what your habits are. Bad habits put you at a decided disadvantage, regardless of what you do the rest of the time. You might have the noblest intentions to honor God or be a person of character, but bad relational, financial, or physical habits can hold you back. If it's true that 45 percent of your life is on autopilot, you are already hamstrung in your attempts to live the life you want, because you are working with only 55 percent of your energy, time, and attention. Based on my napkin math—and keep in mind I am terrible at math—if you made every conscious choice to do right, your highest potential "life grade" is a D once your bad habits are subtracted. It's an enormous handicap to overcome.

On the other hand, if you pour healthy habits into concrete, the right choices become automatic. Whatever conscious effort you put in adds to a good foundation. How epic would it be if, before you used an ounce of willpower and made a single decision, you were starting out at 45 percent? You would only have to give 20 percent effort to be at that same D grade that took three times as much work with bad habits.

Bottom line: you don't have to try nearly as hard if you can get your habits to work for you. Your habits either put the wind in your face or at your back. The right ones need to stay, and the wrong ones need to go.

♣ The Bible says that "slack habits and sloppy work are as bad as vandalism" (Proverbs 18:9 MSG). How do you think your bad habits "steal" life from you?

♣ What's a good habit you do daily without much thought? How did you start this habit?

♣ Read Ephesians 4:22–24. What does Paul mean by "your old self"? What are some ways that you can counter the pull to go into autopilot each day with your habits?

♣ At the beginning of this study, you declared war on what holds you back. Take a moment to reflect on your progress. What's been your toughest battle? What's been your greatest victory?

DAY TWO:
FUTURE YOU

The habits you allow in your life today are going to determine who you become tomorrow.

Future you is an exaggerated version of current you. Time doesn't change anything; it merely deepens and reveals who we are. If you are kind today, you will be kinder tomorrow. If you are cruel today, that, too, will deepen. Smile lines or frowning wrinkles are forming on your face at this very moment. Generous old people are people who, when they were young, lived lives of generosity, and cranky old people grew out of young people who never learned to get out of their own way. . . .

Whatever new habits you decide on, make sure to write them down. Those who commit their goals to paper are 42 percent more likely to accomplish them and earn nine times as much over their lifetimes as people who don't. . . .[14]

Know this: it will feel really uncomfortable to jettison behavior that has been with you for a long time. Your desire for comfort will beg you to go back to how it used to be. But you mustn't relent from your declaration of war. I'm begging you.

People who die of hypothermia are often found naked. In their final moments, they were convinced they were hot, so they shed their clothes. What feels right and what is right are often two very different things.

♣ Today's habits determine who you become tomorrow. Base on the current trajectory, how would you describe th future you?

♣ Read Romans 12:21. What habits and actions are you determined to overcome? Declare war against them now.

♣ Have you committed your goals to paper yet? If not, what is your next step for doing so—buying a journal, making time, finalizing your goals? Take time to write them down now.

♣ Read Proverbs 14:12. What does this verse say about what *feels* right and what *is* right. Where have you seen this play out in your life?

DAY THREE:
The Power of Exponential Growth

I came across a fascinating legend about the invention of chess in sixth-century India.[15] Supposedly the inventor who brought it to the king for his approval found that the monarch loved it. The king found this miniature war to be a challenging and puzzling battle of wits and was delighted with it. He rather bombastically told the inventor that he could name his reward, fully expecting him to ask for a bag of gold, land holdings, or perhaps a title.

Instead, with one hand the man reached into a bowl of food on the table and grabbed a handful of grains, and with the other he swept the pieces from the chess board that separated them. Placing one grain on a single square in one of the corners and then two on the second square, he said, "For my reward, I would like to be given grain sufficient to cover this board in this fashion. The third will have twice what is on the second, and so on until all the spaces are filled."

The king was incredulous and, full of pity, he pressed whether the inventor wouldn't prefer a fancy home or expensive horse. When the man indicated that all he wanted was the grain, the king slapped him on the back and decreed that it would be done.

When the inventor departed, the king told the servants to fill the board with food and have it sent to the inventor's home. But once the math was calculated, a trembling attendant brought to the king his notes. There was not enough money in the entire kingdom to finance this debt nor enough grain in all of India to accomplish it. In fact, if the entire surface of the earth were covered in a layer of grain, it would need to be twice as big in order to equal the amount of grain required. How did the sum get so big? The grains of rice compounded one space at a time, and soon it was checkmate. . . .

It is critical that you take seriously the battles you are facing. It might feel like a small thing that you get in fights with your parents that cause you to fly off the handle or that you can't control your anger when provoked by your sister, but if you can't keep your temper in check, down the road you'll be in an adversarial relationship with your boss where you fly off the handle or a marriage where you can't control your anger. The stakes get bigger; the stimuli do not.

♣ How has the power of exponential growth played out (for good or bad) in your finances, your hobbies, or even your health?

♣ Read 1 Timothy 4:12–14. What instructions does Paul give Timothy?

♣ How would you explain the importance of establishing good habits to young adults today? Did you receive similar advice when you were their age? Did it make a difference in your actions?

♣ The right time to do the right thing is *now*. What situatio
are you facing now that requires decisive action? What i
your plan for actively stepping into it with God?

DAY FOUR:
Becoming Unstoppable

It's not getting to the finish line that is the most difficult part
of any journey or undertaking; it's showing up at the starting
line. The dread of beginning is unbearable. The space shuttle
uses more fuel taking off than in the rest of the flight put
together. The hardest part is getting off the ground. . . .

It's simple physics, really. Unless acted on by an outside
force, objects at rest stay at rest and objects in motion stay in
motion. At least that's my recollection of Sir Isaac Newton's
brilliant discovery as he articulated it in the First Law of
Motion. The hardest part is disrupting inertia. Once you put
a new habit into motion, you'll feel the wind at your back.
I'm not minimizing how hard inertia is to overcome; I'm just
reassuring you that, as Teddy Roosevelt discovered, there
is a prize waiting for you on the other side of the barbed
wire—the wolf will rise. . . .

The first few times—and maybe even the first thousand
times—you respond to the old cue in a new way won't be
easy. Full disclosure: it might feel unbearable. But do it long
enough and you will be only a little uncomfortable. Eventually
you'll feel unstoppable. When you commit yourself to the
process, you'll feel like David when he exclaimed, "With your

help I can advance against a troop; with my God I can scale
a wall" (Psalm 18:29 NIV).

    The journey of a million miles has to start somewhere,
and that somewhere is where you plant your shoe on the
ground for the first time and believe that providence will
have your back.

♣ Is stepping up to the starting line or trying to get to the finish
line harder for you? What is the fear or the negative self-talk
that tries to overtake you in that part of your journey?

♣ In Ephesians 5:10, Paul says, "Figure out what will please
Christ, and then do it" (MSG). This verse gives two assign-
ments. Do you struggle most with knowing what Jesus is
inviting you to do (figuring it out) . . . or actually doing it?
Why?

♣ Does overthinking what you need to do cause you to be
overwhelmed before you start? How can leaning in to God
help you overcome this pattern?

♣ What are ways you can move from being uncomfortable
to unstoppable as you replace negative habits with God-
pleasing ones?

♣ What habit feels like a towering wall that only God can
topple? Have you raised the white flag and asked him to do
that yet? If not, what are you waiting for?

DAY FIVE:
The Private Side of Public Victories

I will never speak without going through an important ritual.
I kneel in prayer and admit my weaknesses so that I can
enter into Christ's strength. You can't rise like a lion if you
don't first kneel like a lamb. There are also very specific
prayers that I pray and words that I speak over myself. . . .

If all this preparation seems like overkill, realize that the
benefit of purposely heightening the intensity before the game
begins is decreased pressure once it does. Remember Alan
Shepard? One fascinating thing he said about that inaugural
flight was how anticlimactic it was. Everyone had worked
so hard to prepare him for the rigors of the launch—he
completed 120 test flights—they had unintentionally *over-*
prepared him. He kept waiting for it to get crazy, but it

was underwhelming in comparison to what he had done in preparation. Engineers had put more G-force generating capability into the centrifuge he trained on than the rocket actually generated. The speakers they put next to his head with recordings of rocket engines were much louder than what he experienced being locked in a sealed capsule that muffled the sounds outside. He said his cooling fan was one of the loudest noises he heard.

We're tempted to phone it in while merely practicing and really turn it on when it is game time: *I'll work hard to prepare a message when the Bible study is not just for a small youth group. I'll memorize the songs instead of reading off a music stand when I lead worship at a bigger church. I'll hustle when I get promoted and have more responsibility. I'll write if and when I get a book deal.*

What Shepard discovered was that the more stress applied to your training, the less you'll stress when it is time to shine. Public victory comes from private discipline. If you aren't busting your butt to kill it where you are, God isn't going to turn up the volume on your life. He isn't going to export to greater platforms what isn't working at home.

♣ **When has advance preparation helped you decrease the pressure of a big event?**

♣ We want shortcuts to long-term success, but that is rarely God's plan. Where have you been coasting as you wait for God to promote you to a new assignment? How has that worked out?

♣ In what area of life are you doing the hard work of pursuing private discipline over public victory? What words would you use to describe this time of pushing through?

♣ Is it difficult to stay with something when it's just you and God working on it and the rewards aren't immediate? Why or why not?

For Next Week

Use the space below to write any key insights or questions from your personal study that you want to discuss at the next group meeting. In preparation for next week, review Card 4 (chapters 11–13) and the conclusion in *I Declare War*.

5

YOUR SECRET WEAPON
IN THE BATTLE

*In the final choice, a soldier's pack is not so
heavy a burden as a prisoner's chains.*

PRESIDENT DWIGHT D. EISENHOWER

Welcome

In the game of War, you have different cards in your deck. You have the card of your thoughts . . . the card of your words . . . the card of your actions. You move through life playing these cards, day by day, and making choices. But it's that fourth card, when there's a tie, that makes all the difference. When you are in a stalemate with your enemy, you need a card of a higher rank to win the battle. You need the card that can't be beaten by any other on your side.

Now, I stand by everything I have given you in the first three cards. Positive thinking is important, and so is watching how you speak and minding your actions. But if that is all you walk away with from this study, I have only given you tools for self-help. Fortunately, there is something better available to you: *God's help*. You have the fourth card—your ace of spades—that you can play in every situation. And it always represents a winning hand.

There is a great scene in *Iron Man 3* where Tony Stark has a malfunction with his suit and crash-lands in a snowy place. He feels claustrophobic and ejects from his suit—but soon regrets the decision when he realizes how cold it is outside. He trudges through the snow, huffing and puffing, carrying the suit behind him like a kid pulling a sled. It's a perfect visual because the suit wasn't designed to be carried by him. It was designed to *carry* him as he executed his calling as a superhero.

The apostle Paul writes that you are created "in Christ Jesus to do good works" (Ephesians 2:10 NIV). *In Christ* is a theological term to describe the way God sees you as being completely

covered in Jesus. But when it comes to fighting battles, you ca
also think of being *in Christ* the way Tony is in the Iron Ma
suit. Through your continued reliance on Jesus, you tap into a
arsenal of protection, ammunition, and navigation. He is you
secret weapon!

So many Christians today are struggling to pull what shoul
propel them. They are trying to fight the battles of this life i
their own strength. They are trying to take back the area tha
the enemy has occupied by relying on their own tactics and strat
egies. Don't make that same mistake! You have the Suprem
Commander of the forces of heaven on your side. So call fo
his firepower, and then be ready to occupy the territory he ha
cleared with the strategies of the first three cards. You have t
maintain what he gives you the power to obtain.

Share

*Begin this final time together as a group by inviting anyone t
share his or her insights from last week's personal study. The
to kick things off, discuss one of the following questions:*

♣ What are some reasons that people choose to "eject out o
the suit" and try to face the battle on their own? What i
generally the result?

—or—

♣ The Holy Spirit is our secret weapon in the fight. To thi
point, has the Holy Spirit been an active part of your lif
with God? If so, how? If not, why not?

READ

Invite someone to read aloud the following passage. Listen for fresh insight and to share any new thoughts with the group through the questions that follow.

So he said to me, "This is the word of the LORD to Zerubbabel: 'Not by might nor by power, but by my Spirit,' says the LORD Almighty.

"What are you, mighty mountain? Before Zerubbabel you will become level ground. Then he will bring out the capstone to shouts of 'God bless it! God bless it!'"

Then the word of the LORD came to me: "The hands of Zerubbabel have laid the foundation of this temple; his hands will also complete it. Then you will know that the LORD Almighty has sent me to you.

"Who dares despise the day of small things, since the seven eyes of the LORD that range throughout the earth will rejoice when they see the chosen capstone in the hand of Zerubbabel?"

ZECHARIAH 4:6–10 NIV

♣ **Zerubbabel had been trying to rebuild the temple for nine years when Zechariah penned these words of encouragment to him. How can these same words encourage you today?**

♣ Is it hard to remember that your battles cannot be won in your own strength? How can you rely on God's power to win the war within?

♣ What does this passage tell you about not discounting the "small things" that lead you to where you want to be?

WATCH

Play the video for session five. As you and your group watch, use the following outline to record any thoughts or key points that stand out to you.

NOTES

All of us, right now, have the power of the Holy Spirit within us. Just as the disciples had their own personal Jesus, we have the Spirit that Christ sent into our hearts.

As Zerubbabel is building the temple, God says, "I myself will be a wall of fire around it" (Zechariah 2:5 NIV). God's wall of protection is not made of stone or brick but his holy fire.

The blueprint for winning the war within is found in this Scripture: "'Not by might nor by power, but by my Spirit,' says the LORD Almighty" (Zechariah 4:6 NIV).

We strengthen our souls by spending time in God's Word, through worship, prayer, serving in church, asking for daily bread, and by proclaiming his will be done rather than our own will.

The message of the gospel isn't *try*. It is *trust*. As you believe, God applies that blood of Jesus to our lives and causes us to be seen as holy before him.

Our reliance on the Holy Spirit allows us to soar like eagles rather than be blown here and there like butterflies. He is our ultimate trump card in this game of War.

Discuss

Take a few minutes with your group members to discuss what you just watched and explore these concepts together.

1. What weakness do the first three cards contain, and what unique power makes this fourth card more essential than the first three combined?

2. Read aloud **John 16:7**. How could it be to the disciples' advantage for Jesus to go away?

3. Read aloud **Acts 2:40–44**. How did the Holy Spirit come through for the disciples? How have you depended on the Holy Spirit for this kind of supernatural power in your life?

4. As Zerubbabel and his people rebuilt the temple, God promised to guard them with walls of fire rather than brick or stone. What walls of protection do you need in the battles you face? Have you asked God to provide them?

5. Even with the best of intentions, we will fall short. What ongoing daily or weekly practices have you established for experiencing God's forgiveness and restoration?

6. The message of the gospel isn't *try* but *trust*. How have you found this to be true in your life? In what areas do you need to trust more in your secret weapon in the fight?

PRAY

Wrap up this final time together with prayer—simply taking a few minutes to talk with God. Here are a few ideas of what you could pray about based on what you discussed in this session:

♦ Thank God for giving you the gift of the Holy Spirit.
♦ Declare that you will no longer rely on your strength for victory.
♦ Ask that God surround you and your loved ones with his walls of protection.
♦ Thank God for cleansing you daily when you repent and ask for forgiveness.
♦ Pray that you will experience more of God's presence through practices that continually draw you closer to him.
♦ Ask God for the power and presence of the Holy Spirit within you.

RESPOND

Every time the enemy confronts you, he is actually showing hi
cards. He is tipping his hand so you can see what really matter
to him. He opposes that which he fears—and he is definitel
afraid of you stepping into your destiny as a child of God. As w
have seen, the best defense against his attacks is a good offense
So this week, when he tries to come at you, choose to rely o
your secret weapon: "Submit yourselves, then, to God. Resis
the devil, and he will flee from you" (James 4:7 NIV). From tha
stance, rise up in the power of the Holy Spirit—and do whateve
the enemy is trying to get you *not* to do with twice as muc
resolve and determination.

SESSION 5

FINAL PERSONAL STUDY

Reflect on the material you've covered during this final week by engaging in any or all of the following between-sessions activities. Journal or jot down your thoughts after each question, and let God use the time to draw you closer to him. Be sure to share with your group leader or group members in the upcoming weeks any key points or insights that stood out to you.

DAY ONE:
DEMOLISHING STRONGHOLDS

In your life, a stronghold is an area in which you have become entrenched in believing something that isn't true, or in doing something you shouldn't be doing, and as a result the enemy has a heavily fortified position in your life. Simply put: it's a constant pull in the wrong direction.

These strongholds can take many forms: pride, anxiety, lust, resentment, jealousy, bitterness, condemnation, shame, physical abuse, substance abuse, addictions, jealousy and covetousness, eating disorders, compulsive behavior, low self-esteem—the list goes on and on.

Are there things that have a really strong hold on you? Things that are constantly pulling you in the wrong direction? Here's how to demolish them. First, *spot them*. Ask God to open your eyes to hidden sins so you can identify them and recognize them for what they are—areas of oppression in which sin has barricaded itself and the enemy has a power position against you. We are all blind to our own blind spots.

Second, *renounce* the thinking or behavior and set your soul against it. This is called repentance. Third, *paint* the target so heaven can blast it with God's supernatural power. Fourth, let your squad in on what has been going on. God alone can forgive, but other people are needed to walk in healing (see James 5:16).

Finally, vigilantly and diligently *build* something in place of the sin so it can never be rebuilt. If you don't follow up your new start with a new plan, the stronghold will be taken again, and it will be seven times worse than the first time. Getting triple-bypass heart surgery is only effective if the patient exercises and follows a low-cholesterol diet afterward. Otherwise he ends up right where he was before the surgery.

♣ A stronghold can be defined as "a constant pull in the wrong direction." What stronghold has a fortified position in your life? How has it pulled you from God?

♣ Which of the five steps for breaking strongholds seems the hardest to you? Why?

♣ Read Galatians 5:7–9. In this passage, Paul warns against making even small compromises—noting that just a little bit of yeast can work its way through the whole batch of dough. In what ways are you resisting new temptations from the enemy?

♣ When you break a stronghold, the enemy will tempt you in that same area because he knows it worked before. What is your game plan for staying free of the stronghold?

DAY TWO:
Names Matter

I heard recently that the TV show *MythBusters* was originally called *Tall Tales or True*, but the show was rejected when it was pitched to the Discovery Channel. It wasn't until it got the name *MythBusters* that it was given the green light.[16]

Words matter. God has given us a name that is above every name, and his appointed power floods in when we use it. Omitting it is a huge mistake. . . .

David understood what is possible when you are willing to call in God's help as you declare war on all that holds you back. . . . As a young man, he had walked into the valley of Elah to uproot a giant named Goliath who had been blaspheming God for forty days. Everyone in Israel cowered in response to this great enemy who was entrenched in his superiority over them. David was a lot like a horseback rider going up against a tank as he walked up to fight this man of war with only a slingshot and a shepherd's staff. It seemed he was outgunned in every way.

Goliath roared in rage, saliva flying from his grotesque lips as he promised to paint the ground red with David's blood. But David didn't trust in the weapons in his hands; he painted Goliath red by invoking "the name of the Lord of hosts, the God of the armies of Israel" (1 Samuel 17:45 NKJV).

When you fight your battles in the name of Jesus, your enemies won't have any more power over you than the giant did over David that day in the Valley of Elah. As Goliath's corpse hit the earth, and the dust settled, it was evident that even with his 125-pound coat of armor, enormous javelin, spear, and helmet, Goliath was the one who brought the horse to the tank fight.

♣ Read Ephesians 1:3. Do you know these blessings that God has waiting for you? How will taking advantage of them alter your battle plans?

♣ Read Matthew 26:41. Prayer is a weapon that turns off the darkness. In what ways have your prayers led to personal or public victory?

♣ Read Philippians 2:10. What does this passage say about praying in the power of Jesus's name?

♣ Read Ephesians 6:10–18. Have you tried to fight spiritual battles using only human strategies and your own strength and insights? How did that work for you?

DAY THREE:
SECOND WIND

Have you ever said under your breath, *This is too hard; it's more than I can bear*? If so, you're right. You can't. . . .

If you haven't yet faced anything so hard it pushed you to the absolute breaking point, your day will come. I don't mean that disrespectfully; it's just a fact. If you live long enough to love deeply, you will hurt significantly. Everyone has a breaking point, no matter how gallant or brave or strong. Even the very thing keeping you alive—your breath—is limited. . . .

That's why it is so important that you don't try to fight these battles in your own strength or by relying on your own lung power. When your breath is taken away, you need to rely on God for a second wind. The first wind is your natural air given to you at creation, when God breathed into the dust he formed us out of. The second wind is the power of the Holy Spirit given to us after Jesus rose from the dead. . . .

I understand if your antenna shoots up when I bring up the Holy Spirit. But stay with me; this isn't cultish or denominational—it's scriptural. This is an area in which there has been plenty of abuse, but neglect is abuse too. And neglecting the Holy Spirit is like declining the offer of a friend with a truck to help you move, and instead opting to drag your furniture by yourself down the road.

The Holy Spirit is the secret to victorious living. He wants to turbocharge your efforts to live for God and help you prevail in the war with the version of you that you don't want to be. All you have to do is ask God to give you strength, and he will come upon you like a mighty rushing wind, propelling you to places you could never go otherwise. This is the key to being the mom you always wanted to be, handling conflict with your father like you wish you could, being a real-estate agent who is great at your job, and bravely going through chemotherapy like a bright, shining light. I want you to know about his strength so that you don't quit thinking right, speaking right, and doing right.

♣ What experience has pushed you to your breaking point? How did you experience God in new ways as you came to the end of yourself?

♣ A. W. Tozer said, "In most Christian churches the Spirit is quite entirely overlooked. Whether He is present or absent makes no real difference to anyone."[17] Why do you think so many believers are unfamiliar or uncomfortable with the Holy Spirit?

♣ Read Acts 1:8. What promise does Jesus give you in this verse? Have you been "fueled" for service in this way? If not, will you ask God to fill your life with the Holy Spirit right now?

♣ **In what ways could the Holy Spirit serve as a mighty rushing wind in your life, propelling you to places you could never go otherwise?**

DAY FOUR:
Phantom Power

Audio technicians deal with something called phantom power—the ability to send power to certain devices from the soundboard. Certain types of microphones require phantom power in order to function. The phantom power must be specifically turned on for that channel if you want to hear your voice.

Ephesians 4:7 tells us about God's phantom power: "To each one of us grace was given according to the measure of Christ's gift" (NKJV). God, the master soundman, will never hand you a gift and call you to do something without also being willing to give you the electricity to power the gift. Bottom line: you can't win the war within without asking God every day to energize your efforts and then being sensitive to the cues he gives you along the way. Like the rumble strip on the side of the highway, God directs us through gentle nudges to correct our courses.

No matter what God calls you to do, his command comes with enablement. The air force doesn't expect you to bring your own F-16; they give you all you need to fulfill your orders. You also don't need to understand how you're going

to complete your mission. You just need to say okay and
then obey. . . .

Decide to obey God and then let him work out the details.
"Trust in the Lord with all your heart and lean not on your
own understanding. In all your ways acknowledge Him, and
He shall direct your paths" (Proverbs 3:5–6 NKJV). The end
result will be that you see him magnificently work things
out, but first you have to take the gutsy step of faith that
says, *I believe.*

He's got the power; you just need to ask for it. He is a
good Father. He won't give you a tarantula if you ask for a
Fruit Roll-Up. But he will give you the Holy Spirit if you ask
him to.

♣ Write Ephesians 4:7 in the space below. How does this passage reveal what God is up to in your life? What is your role
in partnering with him?

♣ Are you sensitive to the cues of the Holy Spirit as you go
through each day? When is the last time you sensed his
nudging and altered your plans because of it?

♣ Read Matthew 19:26. No matter what God calls you to do, he always enables you to do it. How has God come through for you to make seemingly impossible situations possible?

♣ Read Psalm 56:3–4. Do you find it hard to obey God when you are afraid? Do you trust him with no upfront guarantees? Why or why not?

DAY FIVE:
The Ace of Spades

Ultimately the war we have been talking about is the quest to eliminate idolatry. At the end of the day, all of our problems are worship problems. Our love of attention makes us value other people more than we value Jesus. Our love of stuff means we worship possessions more than Jesus. Our struggles with boldness cause us to worship comfort more than Jesus. . . .

To win the battle, we must tear down the things that have been erected where only God belongs, in the preeminent place of honor, value, and glory. It is a daily battle to continue to put God on the throne and banish the would-be kings, but it's also the only way to get out of your own way, to stop sabotaging yourself, and to lay hold of victory.

You might have seen images of marines in Vietnam with ace of spades playing cards in their helmets. US troops heard that Viet Cong soldiers were superstitious about the spade symbol and saw it as a bad omen to encounter it by chance. So it became common practice to leave an ace of spades on the bodies of killed Vietnamese and even to litter the forested grounds and fields with the card in an attempt to spook them and avoid a firefight. . . . Worship doesn't just win the war—worship is the war. . . .

One last quick piece of advice before you go: A boxing instructor once explained the difference between a *cross* (in which you hit hard with a straight punch) and a *jab* (in which you throw a fast, light punch that is more distracting than damaging). She said something that I think will put you in the right mind-set as you rise up as the nurturing warrior wolf you were born to be: "The jab keeps them busy, but the cross is your power."

♣ Read Luke 4:8. Have you considered the root of all your problems is a *worship* problem? How will knowing this change your understanding of—and approach to—worship?

♣ Where have you been directing your worship other than to God? Is it primarily toward people and their opinions, material objects, or perhaps comfort or control? Name these idols below as a first step to eliminating them.

♣ Read 1 John 1:9. Will you now renounce those idols, asking God to forgive and cleanse you for giving them a place of worship that only God deserves? Write your prayer to God below.

♣ Worship doesn't just win the war . . . worship *is* the war. How does viewing worship in this way change your approach to overcoming the war raging within you?

LEADER'S GUIDE

hank you for your willingness to lead your group throug[h] this study! What you have chosen to do is valuable an[d] will make a great difference in the lives of others. The reward[s] of being a leader are different from those of participating, an[d] we hope that as you lead you will find your own walk with Jesu[s] deepened by this experience.

I Declare War is a five-session study built around video con[-]tent and small-group interaction. As the group leader, just thin[k] of yourself as the host of a dinner party. Your job is to take car[e] of your guests by managing all the behind-the-scenes details s[o] that when everyone arrives, they can just enjoy time together.

As the group leader, your role is not to answer all the ques[-]tions or reteach the content—the video, book, and study guid[e] will do most of that work. Your job is to guide the experienc[e] and cultivate your small group into a kind of teaching commu[-]nity. This will make it a place for members to process, question[,] and reflect—not receive more instruction.

Before your first meeting, make sure everyone in the grou[p] gets a copy of the study guide. This will keep everyone on th[e] same page and help the process run more smoothly. If som[e] group members are unable to purchase the guide, arrange it s[o] that people can share the resource with other group members[.]

Giving everyone access to all the material will position this study to be as rewarding an experience as possible. Everyone should feel free to write in his or her study guide and bring it to group every week.

Setting Up the Group

You will need to determine with your group how long you want to meet each week so you can plan your time accordingly. Generally, most groups like to meet for either sixty minutes or ninety minutes, so you could use one of the following schedules:

Section	60 minutes	90 minutes
Welcome (members arrive and get settled)	5 minutes	5 minutes
Share (discuss one or more of the opening questions for the session)	5 minutes	10 minutes
Read (discuss the questions based on the Scripture reading for the week)	5 minutes	10 minutes
Watch (view the video teaching together and take notes)	15 minutes	15 minutes
Discuss (discuss the Bible study questions you selected ahead of time)	25 minutes	40 minutes
Prayer/Respond (pray together as a group and dismiss)	5 minutes	10 minutes

As the group leader, you'll want to create an environment that encourages sharing and learning. A church sanctuary or formal classroom may not be as ideal as a living room, because those locations can feel formal and less intimate. No matter what setting you choose, provide enough comfortable seating for everyone, and, if possible, arrange the seats in a semicircle so everyone can see the video easily. This will make transition between the video and group conversation more efficient and natural.

Also, try to get to the meeting site early so you can greet participants as they arrive. Simple refreshments create a welcoming atmosphere and can be a wonderful addition to a group study evening. Try to take food and pet allergies into account to make your guests as comfortable as possible. You may also want to consider offering childcare to couples with children who want to attend. Finally, be sure your media technology is working properly. Managing these details up front will make the rest of your group experience flow smoothly and provide a welcoming space in which to engage the content of *I Declare War*.

Starting the Group Time

Once everyone has arrived, it's time to begin the group. Here are some simple tips to make your group time healthy, enjoyable, and effective.

First, begin the meeting with a short prayer and remind the group members to put their phones on silent. This is a way to make sure you can all be present with one another and with God. Next, give each person a few minutes to respond to the questions in the "Share" and "Read" sections. This won't require as much time in session one, but beginning in session two, people will need more time to share their insights from their personal studies. Usually, you won't answer the discussion questions yourself, but you should go first with the "Share" and "Read" questions, answering briefly and with a reasonable amount of transparency.

At the end of session one, invite the group members to complete the between-sessions personal studies for that week. Explain that you will be providing some time before the video teaching next week for anyone to share insights. Let them know sharing is optional, and it's no problem if they can't get to some of the between-sessions activities some weeks. It will still be beneficial for them to hear from the other participants and learn about what they discovered.

LEADING THE DISCUSSION TIME

Now that the group is engaged, it's time to watch the video and respond with some directed small-group discussion. Encourage all the group members to participate in the discussion, but make sure they know they don't have to do so. As the discussion progresses, you may want to follow up with comments such as, "Tell me more about that," or, "Why did you answer that way?" This will allow the group participants to deepen their reflections and invite meaningful sharing in a nonthreatening way.

Note that you have been given multiple questions to use in each session, and you do not have to use them all or even follow them in order. Feel free to pick and choose questions based on either the needs of your group or how the conversation is flowing. Also, don't be afraid of silence. Offering a question and allowing up to thirty seconds of silence is okay. It allows people space to think about how they want to respond and also gives them time to do so.

As group leader, you are the boundary keeper for your group. Do not let anyone (yourself included) dominate the group time. Keep an eye out for group members who might be tempted to "attack" folks they disagree with or try to "fix" those having struggles. These kinds of behaviors can derail a group's momentum, so they need to be steered in a different direction. Model active listening and encourage everyone in your group to do the same. This will make your group time a safe space and create a positive community.

The group discussion leads to a closing time of prayer and individual reflection. Take a few moments to pray as a group, and then encourage the participants to review what they've learned and write down their thoughts, if requested, to the "Respond" section. This will help them cement the big ideas in their minds as you close the session.

Thank you again for taking the time to lead your group. You are making a difference in the lives of others and having an impact on the kingdom of God.

Endnotes

1. Franklin D. Roosevelt, "Address to Congress Requesting a Declaration of War with Japan," December 8, 1941, transcript available at http://www.presidency.ucsb.edu/ws/?pid=16053.

2. John Wertheim, "San Francisco's Leaning Tower of Lawsuits," *60 Minutes*, aired November 5, 2017, CBS, transcript available at https://www.cbsnews.com/news/san-franciscos-leaning-tower-of-lawsuits/.

3. Theodore Roosevelt, "A Colonial Survival," *The Cosmopolitan* 14 (November 1892–April 1893), 232.

4. Edmund Morris, *The Rise of Theodore Roosevelt* (New York: Random House, 2001), 674.

5. William Hutchison Murray, *The Scottish Himalayan Expedition* (London: J. M. Dent, 1951), 7.

6. Winston Churchill, *London to Ladysmith via Pretoria* (London: Longmans Green, 1900).

7. Jocko Willink and Leif Babin, *Extreme Ownership: How US Navy SEALs Lead and Win* (New York: St. Martin's Press, 2015), 199.

8. "This Day in History: September 2, 1666," *History.com*, https://www.history.com/this-day-in-history/great-fire-of-london-begins.

9. Nsikan Akpan, "8 Things You Didn't Know About Orville

Wright," *Science*, August 20, 2015, https://www.pbs.org/newshour/science/8-things-didnt-know-orville-wright.

10. Emmie Martin, "How This Graffiti Artist Made $200 Million Overnight," *CNBC*, September 7, 2017, https://www.cnbc.com/2017/09/07/how-facebook-graffiti-artist-david-choe-earned-200-million.html.

11. Will Durant, *The Story of Philosophy: The Lives and Opinions of the World's Greatest Philosophers from Plato to John Dewey* (New York: Pocket, 1953), 76.

12. Daniel Goleman, Richard Boyatzis, and Annie McKee, "Primal Leadership: The Hidden Driver of Great Performance," in *Everyday Emotional Intelligence: Big Ideas and Practical Advice on How to Be Human at Work* (Cambridge: Harvard Business Review, 2018), eBook.

13. David T. Neal, Wendy Wood, and Jeffrey M. Quinn, "Habits—A Repeat Performance," *Current Directions in Psychological Science* 15, no. 4 (2006), 198.

14. Mary Morrissey, "The Power of Writing Down Your Goals and Dreams," *Huffington Post*, updated December 6, 2017, https://www.huffingtonpost.com/marymorrissey/the-power-of-writing-down_b_12002348.html; Mark Milotay, *Practical Goal Setting: A Guide for Real People Who Want to Live Unreal Lives* (CreateSpace, 2013), 5–6.

15. Nikola Slavkovic, "A Piece of Paper as Big as the Universe!," June 10, 2014, YouTube video, 2:34, https://www.youtube.com/watch?time_continue=69&v=AAwabyyqWK0.

16. Gary Strauss and USA Today, "MythBusters Is the Stuff of Legends, Tall Tales," *ABC News*, January 20, 2008, https://abcnews.go.com/Technology/story?id=4160444&page=1.

17. A.W. Tozer, "The Holy Spirit: Present or Active?" cited in *Tozer on The Holy Spirit* (Chicago: Moody, 2000), reading for January 3.